How To Start Green Home Computing

HowExpert Press

Copyright www.HowExpert.com

Visit www.HowExpert.com for FREE TIPS!

Table of Contents

Chapter 1: Introduction To Green Home Computing

In the world of information technology, green computing is defined as the use of computer and its resources in a responsible and eco-friendly manner. The aim of getting greener can be achieved in computing by making the environmentally responsible selection of technology and learning the right way to use the computer and to dispose of the useless computing devices in protected way.

Users can make their houses and work places greener by minimizing the energy consumption of computer systems and its peripheral devices. In addition, reduce in electronic waste amount of computer system helps a lot to go greener.

Many IT vendors have continuously inventing techniques to introduce the eco-friendly servers, laptops, desktop computers and power proficient peripheral devices.

In a precise way, green computing is a systematic study discipline for designing, producing, utilizing, disposing and effectively recycling of computing items to achieve environmental sustainability and reducing the dangerous impact on the environment.

Aims Of Green Computing

- Using the computing devices in an efficient manner for minimizing power consumption.
- Appropriate disposal of redundant computer items and try to reuse and upgrade the old computers.
- Manufacturing and using eco-friendly computing equipment.
- Do computer manufacturing while having nominal effect on the environment.

Chapter 2: What The Guide Focuses On

In this globalized era, people recognize the importance of environmentally friendly and green home appliances. It is highly important to conserve the energy resources and develop the ways to make use of scarce resources in a proper way. Green computing guides the user to make an eco-friendly use of computers and discourage the disastrous use of technology.

Green home computing helps the home individuals to save money and gets benefitted with a safe experience. This guide will help you to follow simple tactics to build an energy efficient and low cost personal green computer. The resourceful contents of this guide will also enable the user to make a smarter use of printer inside the house and how a computer can be recycled and disposed off in a protected way.

Chapter 3: Make Your Computer Green

INSTALL ENERGY EFFICIENT OS

User should go for the lower energy operated software for becoming eco-friendly. The updated version of Windows operating systems like Window 7 is equipped with smart memory management, Disk Input/output cycles and processing methods; and therefore it uses less energy in comparison to other OS versions and is environmentally greener.

USE SMALL SIZE HARD DISK DRIVE

Power consumption also depends upon the size of hard disk. SSD (Solid State Drive) makes use of less power in contrast to the mechanical hard disk because its working relies on the use of flash memory.

AVOID EXTERNAL GRAPHIC CARDS

Home users generally do not need highly specialized graphics. For this reason, you should avoid the use of such peripheral items to save money and electricity.

Avoid Hi-Fi Sound Cards And PCI LAN Cards

The sound cards and PCI LAN cards with many features consume a lot of energy, so you should avoid the use of such high-tech items. A home user should only choose a PCI LAN card if he or she has a real need for it.

Regularly Clean Your Computer

Users should clean their computers at regular intervals to remove debris and dust around CPU fans, plugs, SMPS, etc. This will eliminate overheating and reduce power consumption.

To clean your computer, follow these steps:

- Use a hand-held vacuum cleaner to clean the externals of the computer.
- Use small compressed air bursts to clean inside the computer.
- Use a line-free piece of cloth or tweezers or an air compressor for cleaning the cables, slots and plug heads.

Employ USB Sticks And An External Hard Drive

Instead of storing large amounts of data on the computer, it is better to use external hard disk drives and USB memory sticks. This will not only save computer space, it will maximize the performance of the computer.

UPGRADE COMPUTER HARDWARE

For going green and reducing the e-waste, it is better to upgrade the existing computing system rather than purchasing an entirely new system. The user can optimize the efficiency of his computer system by adding extra RAM or a hard drive.

TUNE YOUR COMPUTER REGULARLY

With the passage of time, a computer needs proper maintenance just like any other electronic appliances. A fully tuned PC is energy efficient and can perform in such a dynamic way that it reduces heat, electricity consumption and the time it takes to perform a task. This increases the life of the computer system and serves the user in an eco-friendly way.

Some useful tactics to maintain your system are as follows:

DEFRAGMENT THE HARD DRIVE

- Double click on **My Computer** from the computer desktop.
- Right click the hard drive from the opening window and click on **Properties**.

Computer Window

- Choose the *Tools* tab from the next open window and select the *Defragment Now* option.

Hard Drive Properties Window

Hard Drive Window

- From the screen which appears next, again select the drive that is fragmented from the list and click on **Defragment Disk**.

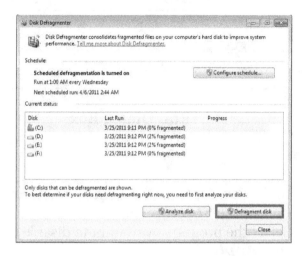

Disk Defragmenter Window

DISABLE UNNECESSARY STARTUP PROGRAMS

When the user starts up a computer system, many unwanted program items begin to load into the memory that slow down the computer system.

The user can disable such processes by following the steps below:

- Click on the Run option from the **Start** menu.
- In the **Open** field, type '**msconfig**' and click on Ok.

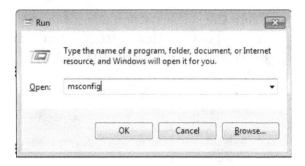

Run Dialog Box

- In the next *System Configuration* window, Choose the *Startup* tab.
- Select the programs you want to disable and click *Apply*.

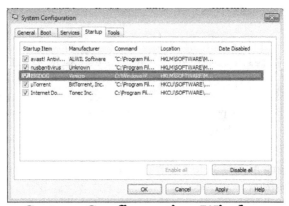

System Configuration Window

The Internet is the most widely used utility/feature of computing to communicate, play or work. The user can adjust internet settings for better performance by following the steps below:

- **Minimizing Storage Of Web Page History**

    o Open ***Internet Explorer*** and click on the ***tools*** menu.

Internet Explorer Window

    o Click on ***Internet Options*** from the drop down list.

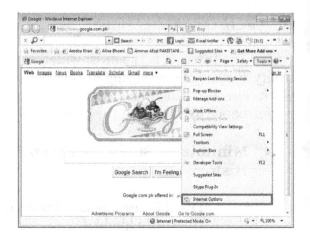

Internet Explorer Window

o From the opening window, select the *General* tab and then click on the *Settings* button under the *Browsing History* option.

Internet Option Window

o Under the ***History option***, choose ***1*** in the box labeled ***Days to keep pages*** in history and click ***OK***.

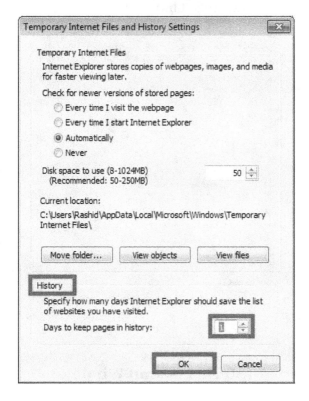

Temporary Internet Files and History Settings Window

- ## Stop the Saving Of Encrypted Pages

  - o Open *Internet Explorer* and click on the *Tools* menu.
  - o Click on *Internet Options* from the drop-down list.
  - o From the opening window, select the Advanced tab.

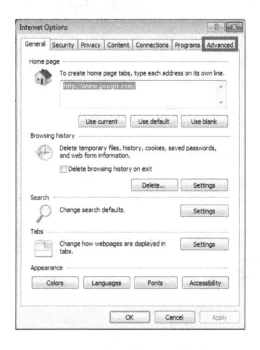

Internet Option Window

  - o Under the *Settings* section, scroll down the list up to the *Security* section part.

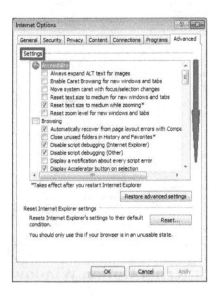

Internet Option Window

o Under the *Security* portion, check the option labeled ***Do not save encrypted pages to disk*** and click *OK.*

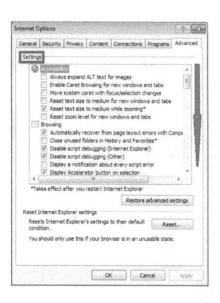

Internet Option Window

ENCOURAGE THE USE OF DOWNLOADABLE SOFTWARE

The user should make extensive use of downloadable software rather than purchasing software at the store or ordering it for home delivery. This practice will save you time and reduces the need for packaging, which helps the environment.

PLANT A TREE

Users should plant at least one tree to reduce the CO_2 emission of the computer equipment they have purchased. Some vendors like Dell have introduced a program "Plant a Tree for Me" to help initiate their customers into this campaign to stop global warming.

MAKE USE OF YOUR COMPUTER FOR TV

Many people share the habit of watching television while working on the computer systems. The user can use their computer system for both purposes, thus reducing the need for a television in the house, which reduces electrical consumption and waste. Additionally, the user can play games, video or music on a single device such as the computer system while working.

You can configure your computer system for TV service by following these steps:

- For this, you must have TV compatible output in the computer such as an S-Video jack.
- Connect the computer system with the TV via an S-Video cable. Alternatively, the user can use a VGA to S-video cable or employ a VGA to component video cable for connecting the VGA adapter end to the computer. The user also needs to have an RCA or component cable to link the TV.
- After making all the connections, examine the TV video input. Press the input button and observe the computer signals.
- The user can activate the TV service from the Control Panel by selecting *Display*.

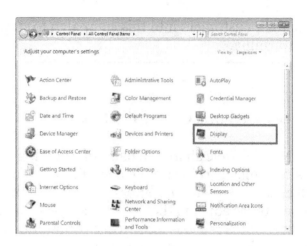

Control Panel Window

- In the next window that opens, select the option labeled *Change Display Settings*.

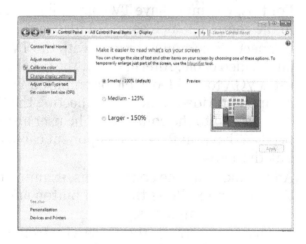

Display Settings Window

- From the next window that opens, click on the **Detect** button to detect the TV screen. The user can set the two different displays from both the computer and TV, or mirror each display on the other.

Screen Resolution Window

Note: The user can quite easily watch live TV programs directly from the Internet via software streaming solutions.

Maintain Appropriate Working Conditions

Computers get hot when used for long periods of time and become uncomfortable to operate without an air conditioner. Instead of utilizing AC, use the room air exhaust system or simply open the window to create comfortable working conditions around computer systems.

Chapter 4: Purchase A Green Computer And Peripheral Devices

ESTIMATE YOUR NEEDS FIRST

Many users think it is necessary to purchase state-of-the-art, fancier computer equipment every couple of years. If you are concerned about green computing, you should carefully estimate your working needs before buying a new computer. Picking physically smaller computers and peripherals that use less energy is better for the environment and your wallet.

BUY A LAPTOP

The average laptop computer uses on average only 15 watts of power and is equipped with a wide range of power management features. Contrast this with desktop computers, which consume around ten times more power than a laptop and have far few power management options. You can possibly save as much as 90% on energy use just by substituting laptops in place of typical desktop computers.

PURCHASE AN ENERGY EFFICIENT DESKTOP

There are many users around the globe who wants to stick with classic desktop computers. For such users, many IT vendors have introduced green computing items like lower rated power suppliers, intelligent and passive cooling configurations, energy efficient system processors, etc. Such devices are usually labeled with the ENERGY STAR® logo image.

GO FOR A FLAT SCREEN DISPLAY

In today's modern era, there is a trend to purchase smart and small display devices. Such displays are energy efficient and generally do not cause eye strain problems.

PURCHASE AN EXTENSIVELY WARRANTED SYSTEM ITEMS

Whether building an entirely new green system or upgrading existing systems, it is beneficial to stick to computing systems that offer long warranties. By purchasing items with long warranties, the user does not need to be troubled by expensive repair problems and can avoid work schedule inconvenience.

BUY COMBINED AND SMART PERIPHERAL ARRANGEMENTS

While purchasing computing items, it is best to select combinations of computing items. Many manufacturers are now marketing smart arrangements of peripheral devices such as combined scanners and printers or combined photocopiers and printers. These smart devices require only a single power supply, hence they result in power saving.

CHOOSE ITEMS WITH LESS PLASTIC WRAP

If you are concerned about making your environment greener, purchase computing items from manufacturers who use less plastic and other hazardous material in packaging computing equipment. In general, the less packaging there is the better.

PURCHASE CERTIFIED HARDWARE DEVICES

RoHS and EnergyStar are the well-known certifications for computer hardware items. RoHS-certified hardware equipment contains a nominal amount of mercury, cadmium, lead and other toxic chemicals, while EnergyStar certified devices are energy efficient. Choosing electronic items with these labels is safer, both for you and for the environment.

Chapter 5: Green Computing Recycling And Disposing

Recycling is one of the best practices to reduce electronic waste. It is highly important to properly recycle or dispose of electronic devices in order to have the least impact on the environment. This section will teach the user a variety of ways to recycle and dispose of computing equipment with reducing electronic waste in mind.

Before disposing, recycling or donating, it is important to backup all important data and examine whether devices can be recycled or reused or not.

SEND BACK TO MANUFACTURING COMPANY

Many IT venders like Intel, IBM, Apple, HP, Dell, etc. have started their own computer recycling and "Take Back" programs. The user needs to simply send back the computer or its peripheral devices to the company. Such companies have the techniques to break down or recycle useless items under controlled conditions.

DONATE OR RESELL THE OLD COMPUTER

If your computer is still working, then the best option for getting rid of a computer system is to donate it to some non-profit organization. The user may also be able to resell the computer system to make some money and to help those people who cannot afford a new one.

LOOK FOR RECYCLING COMPANIES

With a little effort, you should have no problem finding non-profit recycling companies in your area. These companies specialize in recycling activities and do it for free.

PURCHASE A REFURBISHED COMPUTER

When it is time to upgrade your computer system, consider purchasing second hand or renovated computers. You can easily find a good quality refurbished computer by making a little bit of effort to look around the marketplace.

Chapter 6: Practice Efficient Computer Power Management

A regular desktop computer consumes around 60-5000 watts of power on average, and a computer with an LCD screen may consume 35-135 watts of electricity. This section will equip the user with energy-saving techniques that will help the environment.

A brief elaboration of energy efficient and green tools is as follows:

Choose A Superlative PSU

Many manufacturers now aim to design a PSU or power supply unit that supplies power only when it is required, thus minimizing the use of electricity when the PC is idle. Recent PSUs are more than eighty percent energy efficient, because some amount of energy is wasted in the form of noise and heat.

For selecting an optimal power supply unit, the user should look for one that is lead free, RoHS compliant, and 80 Plus-certified.

Don't Use A Screen Saver

A large amount of computer energy is wasted through the monitor. We suggest forgoing the use of a screen saver. Modern computers are equipped with tools to turn off the display automatically after a preset time limit if the computer sits unused.

To turn off the screen saver and utilize the option which automatically turns off the display after a period of disuse, follow these steps:

- Right click on the desktop and choose the *Personalize* option.

Desktop Option

- From window which opens, click on the *Screen Saver* icon option.

Personalize Window

- Click under **Screen Saver** to expand the drop down list.

Screen Saver Settings Window

- Select the ***None*** option and click on the ***Ok*** button to apply the changes.
- Click on ***Control Panel*** from the Start menu.
- Click on ***Power Option*** from the window which opens.

Control Panel Window

- From the left pane of the next window which opens, select the option labeled ***Choose when to turn off the display***.

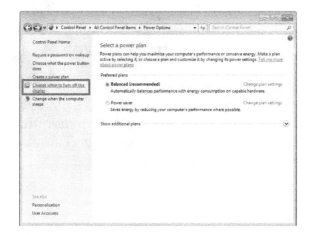

Power Option Window

- In the next window which appears, expand the option ***Turn off the display*** and select a time interval of 10 or 15 minutes. Click on the ***Save changes*** button to apply the changes.

Edit Plan Settings

TURN DOWN THE COMPUTER BRIGHTNESS

It sounds odd to many users that by decreasing computer brightness, you will help save power units, but in reality it happens. Many desktop monitors have dials and buttons to adjust the settings. This also helps you avoid eye strain problems.

MODIFYING POWER SETTINGS

The power option may vary from computer to computer with respect to the hardware configuration that your system supports. The power option feature of Windows automatically perceives the requirements of your computer and shows what is available accordingly.

To set the power option of your computer system, the following steps are involved:

- Click on the **Start** menu and move to the **Control Panel**.

Start Menu

- From the window which opens, choose **Power Option**.
- From the screen which appears next, check the **Power Saver** option under the **Preferred Plan.**

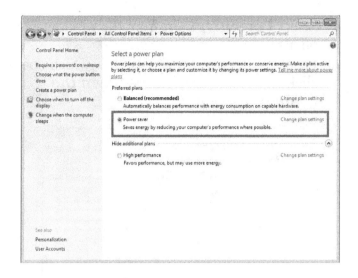

Power Option Window

USE HIBERNATE OR SLEEP MODE

Experts discourage shutting down or turning on the computer several times in a single day. Frequently turning it on or off consumes more power than just keeping it on. Windows offers hibernate or sleep mode options which save the in-progress settings and set the computer to a lower state of energy use.

To choose hibernate or sleep mode settings, the following steps are involved:

- Click on the ***Start*** button and from the menu which opens, select ***Control Panel.***

- Select *Power Option* from the window which opens.
- From the left pane of the window which opens, click on the option *Change when the computer sleeps.*

Power Option Window

- In the next window which appears, select *Change advanced power settings*.

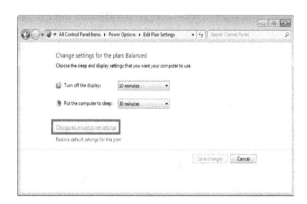

Edit Plan Settings

- In the next Power Options window, expand **Sleep** and adjust the settings to around 20 minutes.

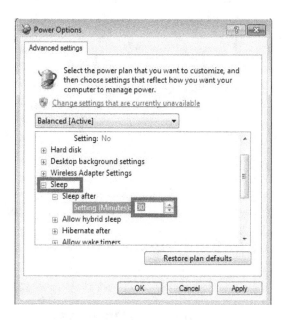

Power Option Window

- Now expand the **Hibernate** option and select the time interval for the hibernate option. Click **Ok** or **Apply** button.

Power Option Window

USE SMALL MONITORS AND DISPLAYS

In general, larger desktop screens use 65 to 250 watts of energy. That is a very high amount in comparison to LCD monitors or a laptop computer screen. Modern LCD monitors are energy efficient and occupy less space. Similarly, laptop computers consume less energy and are considered smarter computing items.

Many IT experts recommend using power strips as a single source for connecting all peripherals in order to cut down "vampire power." It also makes it easier for the user to flip the power switch any time.

SWITCH OFF THE COMPUTER AND OTHER PERIPHERAL DEVICES WHEN THEY ARE NOT NEEDED ANYMORE

Much energy is wasted when the user leaves a computer system on for no reason. You should always properly shut down the computer system when it is not in use. In addition, users should also switch on peripheral devices such as scanners, printers and photocopiers only at the time of immediate need. We also suggest powering off from the main supply source to save power.

INSTALL CO_2 SAVER

CO_2 saver is an online downloadable application program for examining and maintaining the amount of energy your computer consumes. This utility helps the user to reduce the emission of harmful CO_2 and lower electricity usage.

The user can download this application program from the website http://co2saver.snap.com/. The following steps are involved in installing the software:

- Open *Internet Explorer* and type the URL in the address bar.

Internet Explorer Window

- Click on the *Install Now!* button.

CO₂ Web Page

- A dialog box will appear that will let you save the exe file of the software.

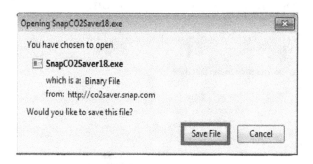

SnapCO₂saver Window

- Now open the exe file directly from the
  Downloads window that will appear
  immediately after downloading the software, or
  go to the *C* drive under *My Computer*.
  Choose *Users* and then select *Downloads*.

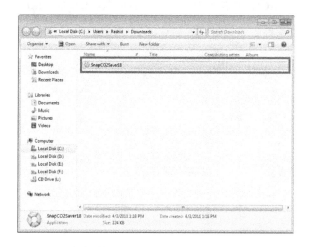

Downloads Folder Window

- Double click on the file and a dialog box will open. Click on the Run option.

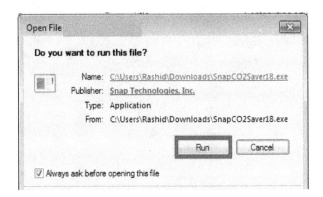

Software Run Option Window

- In the next window which appears, check the box that lets you agree with the terms and conditions that enable you to use the software.

CO₂ Saver Installation Window

44

- Click on the **Finish Installation** button.

Note: the CO_2 Saver automatically configures with the power management settings of your computer system. It activates when the user is away from the computer system after around thirty minutes. However, you can adjust the settings from the option menu that resides in its own setting window placed on the desktop. It also shows the CO_2 emission-saving results to the user.

READ ALL MANUALS

Always carefully read the instructions of the manufacturer's manual that is provided with each computing item. The updated versions of many computing devices are equipped with power management tuning utilities and many equipment manuals give suggestions on how to operate electronic devices in a way to optimally use power.

Chapter 7: Green Computer Printing

Home printers are used in variety of ways at home, including printing reading material, school papers, etc. Although they are useful, they are also environmentally harmful because the used papers come from trees and the printers need electricity to operate. This section will equip the user with good advice for using printers in an eco-friendly, green way.

PRINT ON BOTH SIDES OF THE PAPER

A user should print on both sides of the paper when a document is for personal referencing. Many offices and institutions encourage the use of both sided printing to keep trees and hence the environment safe. Many modern printers can print on both sides of the paper.

The following steps are required to set double-sided printing:

- Click on the **Start** menu and move to the **Control Panel**.
- From the screen which opens, click on **Devices and Printers**.

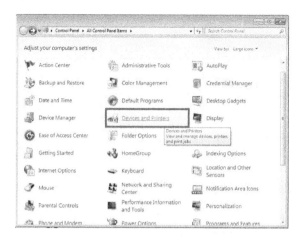

Control Panel Window

- In the window which opens, there will be all printing, webcam, faxing, scanning and other external devices listed. Double click on *Printer*.

Devices and Printer Window

47

- In the next window which opens, select *Adjust print options.*

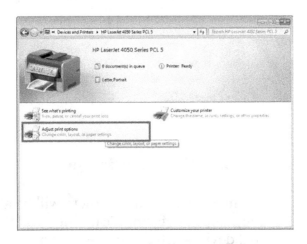

Printer Setting Window

- In the next screen which appears, select the *Finishing* tab.

Printing Preferences Window

- Under ***Document Options***, check the option ***Print on Both Sides*** and click ***OK***.

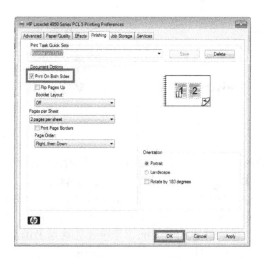

Printing Preferences Window

- The user can also go for even more economical use by selecting two or more than two *Pages per Sheet Option* from the same window.

Printing Preference Window

Note: There may be a slight variation in the steps to follow with respect to which printer you use and your computer system. Many printer vendors provide a booklet with the printer to guide the user on how to install and use the printer. Check the manual if you are presented with different options when trying to perform this step.

Utilize Recycled Paper

One of the best initiatives for green printing is the use of recycled paper. Recycled paper looks similar to normal or regular printing paper but it is economical to use and eco-friendly. Generally, these papers are made from old consumer paper product waste. Many manufacturers employ natural fiber for making eco-friendly printing papers.

Buy Energy Efficient Printers

The latest printers are energy efficient because they use energy properly to print faster. Many companies like HP, Office Max, and Staples have introduced a series of green printers to promote eco-friendly product use. These printers work with automatically power down feature and hence can save the energy up to 50%.

Make Use Of Larger Commercial Printers

Home users do not usually have to print very frequently, so they can make use of kiosk or library printers rather than purchasing their own. These larger printers are more power-efficient and use less energy for printing. These printers are also available in combination arrangements of photocopies and scanner, and so they are more resourceful.

AVOID PRINTING FOR PROOF READING

Many users wrongly print things for proofreading purposes. You should always perform such tasks on the computer by using the spelling and grammar tool of MS Word and other application programs in order to save money, time and paper.

ENCOURAGE THE USE OF SOY AND VEGETABLE INKS

Most cartridge inks contain harmful and dangerous chemical contents that are unfriendly to the environment. An good alternative to these hazardous items is the use of soy and vegetable ink. Several brands of soy and vegetable ink cartridges are available on the market to promote green printing.

USE INK-JET PRINTERS

Although the printing quality of ink-jet printers is not as good as laser printers, they are more power saving. Since home users usually do not have to print in large volumes, ink-jet printers are often sufficient to meet the printing requirements of occasional home users.

RECYCLE PRINTER CARTRIDGES

It is green idea to recycle your printing cartridge rather than to purchase a new one. Many manufacturers offer the ability to mail back the cartridge for recycling by using the envelope that is provided at the time of purchase. Additionally, users can recycle their printer cartridges at home-office-supply stores of many companies like Office Max or Staples.

SUBSCRIBE TO E-NEWSPAPER AND E-NEWSLETTERS

Much paper waste is due to the newspapers and magazines that people throw out every day after reading just once. Many newspaper agencies have electronic editions of newspapers and magazines on their websites. The home user can contribute to the environment in a positive way by reading electronically via email, RSS or on the web.

MAINTAIN DIGITAL SHOPPING RECEIPTS

Printing online shopping receipts persistently can cause more paper wastage than using traditional cash register receipts. The modern and eco-friendly way to maintain receipts is to save digital receipts directly on the computer hard drive or on a portable and smart storage device. Try to practice this!

USE ONLINE FORMS

No matter what the purpose of forms, we suggest filling them out and submitting them online rather than via hard copy.

Chapter 8: Resource Sharing Across Multiple Systems

If you have more than one computer system at home or have a small home network, you can share some peripheral devices among all these computers to save money and reduce e-waste. This section will guide you on how to share a single set of devices across multiple computers.

Some of the most common sharing tactics are as follows:

SHARE A KEYBOARD AND MOUSE

QuickSynergy is a free application program that is used to share a keyboard, mouse and clipboard across multiple systems.

The following steps are involved in installing and using the QuickSynergy software:

- Type http://synergy-foss.org/download in the address bar of Internet Explorer.
- From the page which opens, select the download option that matches your operating system version.
- In the dialogue box which opens, click on the **Save File** button.

QuickSynergy save Option Window

- Double click on the exe file from the folder which contains **Downloads** in the **C** drive.

Downloads Window

- A new opening dialogue will allow you to agree with the terms and conditions. To use this application, Click *I agree* button.

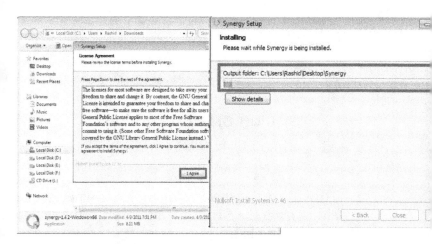

Synergy Startup Window

Synergy Startup Window

- After completing the startup procedure, the user will be directed to specify a destination folder for installation.

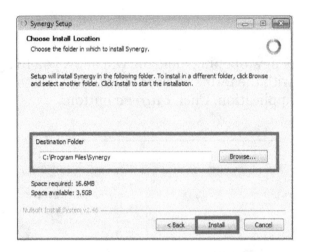

Synergy Startup Window

- To activate the sharing, open QuickSynergy, either from the *Start* menu list or from the *All Programs* list.

Start Menu

- On the server, type the client hostname in the fields under *Use Existing Configuration*, then select the *Start* button to connect.

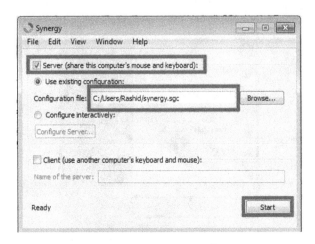

Synergy Window

- On client computer systems, enter the Server IP address under the *Server* tab and then choose the *Start* button.

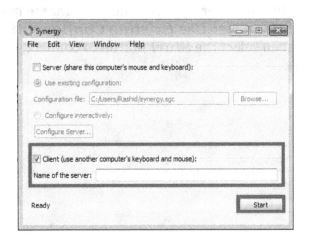

Synergy Window

Conclusion

Green computing has become an exceptionally popular and important phenomenon for the current digitalized era. The responsibility to keep the environment safe is not limited to large organizations, but extends to every single user. Participating in green environment sustainability campaigns really is important.

For domestic home users, the advantages of green computing are quite obvious. Green computer practices help you to minimize the consumption of electricity and reduce heat emissions, thus saving money on installing air conditioning to create bearable working conditions.

There are many solutions available for going green at home. The user can buy a new energy efficient PC or renovate the existing one for better performance. Additionally, you can also promote the environmentally responsible use of computing by proper disposing of useless electronic devices. The environment can also be saved by limiting the use of paper that comes from trees.

Recommended Resources

- **<u>www.HowExpert.com</u>**
  - ○ Get more "How To" guides at our website.